AMAZING CHRISTMAS

FACTS FOR SMART KIDS

300+ FESTIVE FACTS and FUN TRIVIA

BRIGHT MINDS LEARNING

TABLE OF CONTENTS

INTRODUCTION

Hello there, curious reader!

When I think of Christmas, I think of sparkling lights, cozy nights, and the magic of being together with the people we love most. There's something truly special about this time of year that brings out a sense of wonder and excitement in all of us—no matter how old we are. Maybe it's the thrill of seeing the first snowflakes fall, the warmth of baking cookies with family, or the joy of unwrapping gifts on a chilly morning. Christmas is about celebrating the little things that make us happy and sharing that joy with others.

This book is a journey through some of the most fascinating and fun parts of Christmas and winter. From how different countries celebrate around the world to the wonders of the icy Arctic, it's filled with stories that make this season so magical. There are surprises on every page—quirky facts, mind-blowing traditions, and activities that will help you bring a little extra magic into your holidays.

I hope that as you read, you'll find yourself smiling, learning, and imagining. I hope you'll share these stories with your family and friends—maybe while sitting around the tree or snuggled up by a warm fire. And most of all, I hope this book helps you feel the true spirit of Christmas: a time of kindness, wonder, and the magic of believing that anything is possible.

Let's unwrap the magic of Christmas together!

Chapter 1

SANTA CLAUS AND CHRISTMAS SYMBOLS

1. Santa Was Real! (Kind of)

Santa Claus's real name was Saint Nicholas, a kind man from Turkey. The story goes that he gave gifts of money to three girls by secretly dropping sacks through their window to pay for their weddings. Sounds like a real-life Santa, right?

2. Santa's Suit Was Coca-Cola's Idea!

Santa didn't always wear red. In fact, he wore robes in green, purple, blue, and even brown! It was in 1931 when Coca-Cola decided to dress him in the famous red suit for a big ad campaign—and the look stuck!

3. Santa Has Many Names

"Santa Claus" comes from the Dutch "Sinterklaas," which is based on Saint Nicholas. But he's got lots of names around the world: Father Christmas, Kris Kringle, and even Ded Moroz (Grandfather Frost) in Russia!

4. Where in the World Is Santa?

Where does Santa really live? Nobody knows for sure! Some say Finland, others say Greenland, or even Russia. But most believe in the North Pole—the perfect snowy, secret hideaway for a magical guy like Santa!

5. Pilot Santa Takes Flight

Don't worry, Santa won't get stuck in airport security! He was issued a pilot's license by the US government way back in 1927. And in 2013, Canada gave him an official passport, making him an honorary Canadian citizen!

6. Iceland's Thirteen Santas

No Santa Claus in Iceland? No worries! Icelanders have thirteen Santa Clauses called the Yule Lads. They're merry, mischievous, and bring gifts—or rotting potatoes if you've been naughty. Meet Spoon Licker, Sausage Swiper, and their crew—each named for what they do best!

7. Santa's GPS Tracker

Want to see where Santa is? No problem! Thanks to NORAD, you can track Santa's progress across the globe in real time. And they even do it in several languages, so Santa's sleigh is always in the spotlight!

8. The Yule Goat

In Scandinavian folklore, the Yule Goat helped bring gifts, showing how animals have always played a big role in festive traditions.

9. Coal Wasn't Always So Bad

Coal might seem like a crummy gift, but back in the day, it wasn't so terrible. Coal was expensive, and families relied on it for warmth. Even Bob Cratchit from A Christmas Carol could use more coal for his fire, though mean old Scrooge wouldn't let him. Now, we'd prefer a PS5, please!

10. Santa Banned in the Soviet Union!

In 1929, dictator Joseph Stalin banned Christmas, which meant no Santa—or Grandfather Frost as they called him. People still celebrated in secret, though, and Christmas made a comeback in the 1990s when the ban was lifted.

11. Santa's Really, Really Old

Santa Claus is a whopping 1,750 years old! No wonder his beard is so white! He was born in a tiny town called Patara, which is now in modern-day Turkey. Mrs. Claus is younger at a youthful 1,139 years old, and she shares her birthday with Christmas Day—maybe that's why Santa always hurries back home after deliveries!

12. Santa's Sleigh Stats

Santa needs to make 842 million stops on Christmas Eve to deliver all the presents. He travels at an incredible 1,280 miles per second!

13. Santa's Rich List Fame

A business magazine once listed Santa as one of the world's richest people. Who knew delivering joy could be so profitable?

14. The Weight of Santa's Sleigh

Santa's sleigh weighs over 700 million pounds—that's a lot of toys for all the good children!

Imagine This!

What if Santa's reindeer were replaced by different animals from around the world? How would a team of penguins or kangaroos pull Santa's sleigh?

15. Santa Hat World Record

35,000 baseball fans broke the world record for the largest gathering of people wearing Santa hats.

16. Christmas Towns in the USA

There are towns in the USA named Eggnog, Christmas, Mistletoe, Santa Claus, Jolly, North Pole, and Silver Bell. It's Christmas all year long in these places!

17. International University of Santa Claus

There's even an International University of Santa Claus where people can learn the secrets to being the perfect Santa!

18. Santa Helpers Academy

In Finland, you can attend the Elf Training Academy to learn how to be Santa's helper.

19. Santa Marathon in Tokyo

Every year in Tokyo, hundreds of runners dress up as Santa for the city's annual Santa Claus marathon—talk about running with holiday cheer!

20. Santa's Stops in Space

The song "Jingle Bells" was the first song sung in space when astronauts aboard Gemini 6 sang it in 1965.

21. Santa's Ice Maze

In Canada, there's a giant snow maze nearly the size of four professional basketball courts—Santa's team probably loves a good maze!

22. Santa's Tree Farm Thieves

A college in Minnesota, USA, sprays its evergreens with skunk scent to stop people from stealing Christmas trees from its campus—definitely not Santa-approved!

23. Santa and the North Poles

Did you know there are four North Poles? The geographic North Pole, magnetic North Pole, geomagnetic North Pole, and the Pole of inaccessibility.

24. Germany's First Christmas Trees

Christmas trees got their start in Germany over 500 years ago! Families would bring small evergreen trees into their homes and decorate them with apples, nuts, and even candles. This festive German tradition spread around the world, and now millions of families put up and decorate Christmas trees each year!

25. Evergreen Trees Mean Everlasting Life

Christmas trees symbolize everlasting life because evergreens stay green all winter long. Plus, that fresh pine scent comes from oils in the needles that keep bugs away and keep the tree fresh all winter—nature's own magic!

26. From Baby Jesus to Stars and Angels

Originally, the infant Jesus topped Christmas trees. Over time, it evolved into a star or an angel, representing important Christian symbols from the Nativity. Plus, the star on top makes the tree extra sparkly, guiding both Wise Men and our festive hearts!

27. Lights Before the Lights

Christmas tree lights began as real candles, which looked gorgeous but were also a bit dangerous—thank goodness for electric lights that let our trees glow safely today!

28. A Royal Trendsetter

Queen Victoria made Christmas trees super popular in England when she had one at Windsor Castle. It wasn't long before everyone wanted a tree of their own—she really started a royal holiday trend!

29. The Tallest Tree Ever

The tallest Christmas tree ever displayed was in Seattle, standing 221 feet tall—taller than a 20-story building! Nowadays, the Rockefeller Center tree in New York is one of the most famous, dazzling visitors with thousands of lights and a giant star.

30. A Gift From Norway

Each year, Norway gifts a giant Christmas tree to London as a symbol of friendship—now that's a festive way to say "thank you" and keep the holiday spirit alive between nations.

Imagine This!

If you could create your own Christmas tree using anything except pine needles, what would you use? Maybe you'd make a tree out of candy canes, lights, or even snowballs!

31. Christmas Trees Around the World

Christmas trees aren't always fir trees! In New Zealand, the "Pohutakawa" tree with bright red flowers gets decorated, while in India, people sometimes use banana or mango trees—talk about a tropical twist on tradition!

32. Feathery First Fake Trees

Artificial Christmas trees were first made in Germany in the 19th century. Believe it or not, they were made of goose feathers dyed green, attached to wire branches, and wrapped around a rod—pretty creative, right?

33. Thirsty Trees

Even after being cut down, Christmas trees are still thirsty! They can drink almost a liter of water every day during their first week in your home—just like a giant, festive cut flower. So, don't forget to keep your tree hydrated!

34. Tinsel's Shiny History

Tinsel was invented in Germany back in 1610 and was made from real silver—it was definitely a luxury decoration! Today's tinsel may not be made of silver, but it still makes our trees look super festive.

35. The Traveling Christmas Tree

If you buy a Christmas tree from a store, chances are it traveled a lot before it arrived. Most trees grow on farms, and unless you cut it down yourself, it probably spent weeks out of the ground before you decorated it!

36. Pine Cones Are Nature's Humidity Meters

Pine cones aren't just decorations—they're clever too! When the weather is dry, pine cones open up to release their seeds, but when it's humid, they close to protect them. They're like nature's little humidity sensors!

37. Edible Christmas Pine Needles

Did you know that the pine needles of some Christmas trees are actually edible? Varieties like the Eastern White Pine can be used to brew a nutritious tea rich in vitamin C—just be careful which type you nibble on!

38. Mistletoe's Sneaky Secret

Mistletoe stays green all winter because it sneaks minerals and water from its host tree—how clever! Just watch out, though—some species are poisonous, so exactly a friendly plant!

39. Mistletoe as Medicine

Believe it or not, some doctors prescribe mistletoe to help cancer patients manage side effects from chemotherapy. Who knew this cheeky plant had a helpful side?

40. White Berries and Exploding Seeds

Mistletoe berries are actually white, not red—just in case you were picturing little red dots! The dwarf mistletoe's ripe white berries explode, scattering seeds up to 50 feet away. Now, that's one way to spread Christmas cheer!

41. Witches' Brooms for Nesting

Mistletoe makes a great home for birds like mourning doves, spotted owls, and even squirrels. These massive mistletoe clusters, often called "witches' brooms," can weigh up to 50 pounds—perfect for nesting!

42. No Scent for Mistletoe

Mistletoe doesn't have a distinctive smell, which might make you wonder why it's so romantic. It's all about tradition, not the fragrance!

43. Little Dung Twig

The word "mistletoe" means "little dung twig" because birds spread its seeds—yup, kind of gross, but it makes those mistletoe kisses even funnier!

44. Wreaths Are All About Love

Wreaths are made in a circle to symbolize eternity—love and friendship that never end. Just think of them as a giant, leafy hug that lasts forever!

45. The Stocking Legend

Hanging stockings comes from a legend about St. Nicholas dropping gold coins down a chimney—they landed in socks drying by the fire! Originally, they were just plain socks, but today, stockings have gotten way fancier (and much bigger!).

46. An Orange Means Good Luck

Finding an orange in your stocking is a symbol of wealth and prosperity, a reminder of the gold coins left by St. Nicholas. Plus, it makes for a healthy snack!

47. World's Largest Stocking

The world's largest Christmas stocking was made by volunteers in Italy, measuring an incredible 168 feet long and 70 feet wide. It was even stuffed with candy-filled balloons—talk about a super-sized holiday treat!

48. Candy Canes Galore

Candy canes have been a popular stocking stuffer since the late 1800s, and nearly 1.8 billion are made each year. About 90% of them are sold between Thanksgiving and Christmas—so it's no wonder they're a holiday favorite!

49. La Befana's Stocking Tradition

In Italy, kids hang stockings not for Santa, but for La Befana, a kind witch who delivers gifts on Epiphany instead of Christmas Eve. She's like Santa with a magical twist!

50. A Heavy Stocking Tradition

In Holland, kids put out wooden clogs instead of stockings, and if they've been good, they find treats inside. Naughty kids might find a potato instead!

Chapter 2

BIZARRE CHRISTMAS FACTS

1. Jingle Bells' Surprising Origin

"Jingle Bells" wasn't originally a Christmas song—it was written for Thanksgiving! But it soon became one of the most beloved Christmas tunes.

2. Wassailing to Caroling

Caroling started in England as "wassailing," where people sang in exchange for a warm drink—it was like an old-fashioned hot chocolate party! Carols were originally just happy songs people sang during celebrations, not specifically about Christmas.

3. Caroling in the Philippines

In the Philippines, caroling is called "harana." People sing carols to bring good luck and blessings to each household.

4. Christmas Grotto for Penguins

In London, the zoo hosts a special "Christmas Grotto" for penguins, complete with snow and festive decorations. The penguins waddle around enjoying their own little winter wonderland, bringing holiday cheer to all the visitors!

5. Robins on Christmas Cards

Robins are a popular Christmas symbol because of Victorian postmen. Back then, mail carriers were nicknamed "robins," and they started featuring on Christmas cards!

6. The Twelve Days of Christmas

The "12 Days of Christmas" comes from the legend that it took the three kings 12 days to reach baby Jesus. Today, it's a tradition to take down Christmas decorations on the twelfth night—January 6th.

7. The Invisible Christmas Card

The smallest Christmas card ever made is so tiny it's invisible to the human eye! Created by scientists at the University of Glasgow, you need a microscope to see this incredible card.

8. Xmas = Christmas

"Xmas" means the same as "Christmas." The letter 'X' stands for Christ in ancient Greek, so "Merry Xmas" is ancient Greek for Christmas!

9. The First Christmas Card

The first Christmas card was created in 1843 by Sir Henry Cole, showing a family enjoying a festive meal. Little did he know how popular Christmas cards would become!

10. Giant Advent Calendar

The largest Advent calendar ever made was over 200 feet tall, with 24 giant doors—imagine opening one of those each day!

11. The Yule Log's Mythical Roots

The Yule log tradition comes from Norse mythology, where a huge log was burned to bring good luck for the new year. The ashes were kept to protect homes from lightning.

12. The Story of Christmas Crackers

Christmas crackers were invented by a candy maker in London in the 1840s to make his candie more exciting. The crackers "pop" because of small strip of gunpowder inside—don't worry, it's totally safe! The world's longest Christmas cracker was over 200 feet long and was pulled by 40 people!

13. Crowns at Christmas Dinner

In the UK, wearing paper crowns from Christmas crackers is a tradition during dinner, making everyone feel like royalty for the day.

14. Roller Skating to Church

In Caracas, Venezuela, it's tradition to roller skate to church on Christmas Day. It's a fun and unique way to celebrate the season!

15. Christmas in the Sand

In Florida, people make snowmen out of sand since there's no real snow—it's a beachy take on a winter classic.

16. Upside-Down Christmas Trees

In parts of Europe, people used to hang Christmas trees from the ceiling to keep them away from children and pets—an unusual twist on the traditional tree!

17. Christmas Spider Decorations

In Ukraine, people decorate their Christmas trees with fake spiders and webs for good luck—it's a spooky yet festive tradition!

18. Christmas in Ethiopia and Beyond

In countries like Ethiopia, Egypt, Serbia, and Kazakhstan, Christmas is celebrated on January 7th, following the Orthodox calendar.

19. Jumping into Icy Water

In some parts of England, people celebrate Christmas by jumping into icy water—a brave (and very chilly) tradition!

20. Yule Cat Legend

In Iceland, there's a legendary Yule Cat said to eat children who haven't received new clothes for Christmas—talk about a motivation to do laundry!

21. Christmas Tree Species

There are more than 600 species of Christmas trees around the world, with different cultures preferring their favorite variety for the holidays.

22. World's Largest Wreath

The world's largest Christmas wreath was wider than a soccer field and weighed as much as two elephants!

23. Holiday Warning!

Your tongue really can get stuck to a piece of frozen metal - just like in those holiday movies! So, it's best to avoid testing it out.

24. Icicle-Growing Machine

A Canadian scientist developed a machine specifically designed to grow icicles! The machine creates perfect conditions for icicles to form, helping researchers study the science behind these frosty winter decorations.

25. South-Side Icicles

You're more likely to find icicles hanging on the south side of a building than on the north side. That's because the sun shines more directly on the south side, causing snow to melt and refreeze into icicles.

26. Icicle Branches Called Legs

Did you know that the offshoots of an icicle are called "legs"? These branches form as water drips unevenly down an icicle, giving it a leg-like appearance.

27. Record-Sized Snowflakes

On January 10, 1915, Berlin, Germany, experienced a snowstorm with snowflakes measuring up to 4 inches across. These gigantic snowflakes were almost as wide as a person's palm!

28. Christmas Tree Cutting Record

The record for the most Christmas trees chopped down in two minutes is held by an American woman who managed to chop down 27 trees in that short time. Talk about impressive holiday lumberjacking skills!

29. $2 Billion Spent on Wrapping Paper

Americans spend nearly $2 billion every year on wrapping paper alone—just for that satisfying moment of tearing it all off!

30. Christmas Lights Visible from Space

During the holiday season, the brightest Christmas light displays on Earth are visible from outer space. Astronauts aboard the International Space Station have reported seeing the sparkling lights of festive cities from orbit.

31. Chocolate-Scented Fart Pills

A Frenchman invented a Christmas pill that makes your farts smell like chocolate! There's even a powdered version for dogs—perfect for spreading sweet scents during the holidays.

32. Recycled Bottle Christmas Tree

In 2019, a woman in California created a Christmas

tree from over 20,000 recycled water bottles, gaining fame for its beauty and promoting the importance of recycling.

33. Chocolate Christmas Tree in Switzerland

In 2017, a Swiss hotel created an 8,000-pound Christmas tree made entirely of chocolate, decorated with 2,000 chocolate ornaments—a truly sweet holiday display!

34. Life Jacket Christmas Tree at the Vatican

In 2018, the Vatican made a Christmas tree out of old life jackets to raise awareness about refugees and migrants in need of help—adding a meaningful message to the holiday season.

35. Boxing Day in the UK

In the UK, the day after Christmas is called Boxing Day. It's named after the tradition of collecting money in church alms boxes for the poor.

Chapter 3

FESTIVE FOODS AND SWEET TREATS

1. Gingerbread Spice

Gingerbread has been around since Ancient Greece, but it became a popular Christmas treat in Europe during the 16th century—it's the perfect blend of spice and sweetness!

2. The World's Largest Gingerbread House

The largest gingerbread house ever built was a two-story home made with 1,800 pounds of butter, 7,200 eggs, and 3,000 pounds of sugar—sounds delicious!

3. Candy Canes: Keeping Kids Quiet

Candy canes were first made in Germany to keep children quiet during long church services—pretty genius, right?

4. The Shepherd's Staff

The candy cane's shape represents a shepherd's staff, reminding us of the shepherds who visited baby Jesus.

5. Stripes and Peppermint

Originally, candy canes were all white and had no stripes—just sweet sticks! The iconic red stripes were added in the early 20th century, along with the peppermint flavor, giving us the classic candy canes we know today.

6. America's Sweet Obsession

In the United States, over 1.76 billion candy canes are produced each year—that's enough to satisfy every sweet tooth during the holiday season!

Imagine This!

You're designing a new flavor for Christmas cookies. What would it taste like, and what ingredients would you use? Would it be minty, fruity, or maybe something no one has ever tried before?

7. Candy Canes Across the Atlantic

German immigrants brought candy canes to America, sharing their holiday traditions. Now, candy canes come in all kinds of flavors—fruity, sour, and even chocolate—something for everyone!

8. Hot Chocolate Medicine

Once upon a time, hot chocolate was considered a type of medicine—now it's just a cozy holiday treat. The largest cup of hot chocolate ever made could fill 20 bathtubs—it's a hot cocoa lover's dream!

9. Eggnog-Flavored Lip Balm

If you love eggnog, you can even get eggnog-flavored lip balm for a festive twist.

10. World's Largest Candy Cane

The largest candy cane ever made was over 51 feet long—imagine trying to hang that on your tree!

11. European Holiday Sweets

In France, Saint Nicholas rides a donkey loaded with toys for children, and kids leave treats out for the donkey. In Mexico, kids celebrate by breaking a piñata filled with candy.

12. Christmas Treats from Around the World

Kids around the world leave different treats for Santa: sponge cake in Chile, rice pudding in Denmark, meat pies in the UK, coffee in Sweden, and biscuits in France.

13. World's Largest Christmas Pudding

The world's largest Christmas pudding weighed more than a hippo—it was a truly massive holiday dessert!

14. Nativity Scenes Made from Radishes

In some parts of Mexico, people carve Nativity scenes out of radishes—turning vegetables into festive works of art.

15. Jellyfish for Christmas

In Russia, some people celebrate Christmas with a dish called aspic, which is a jelly made from fish or meat. It's definitely not your usual Christmas treat!

16. Meat-Free Polish Feast

During the Christmas Eve feast in Poland, called Wigilia, there are always 12 dishes—but no meat is allowed. Instead, it's all about jellied fish, beetroot soup, and mushroom-filled pierogi.

17. Christmas Pudding Drama

Known for its dramatic flaming presentation, Christmas pudding is set on fire with brandy before serving—talk about a show-stopping dessert!

18. The Eggnog Twist

American eggnog often comes with a splash of rum, while in Puerto Rico, "coquito" adds coconut milk for a tropical twist to the holiday classic.

19. Germany's Fruity Bread: Stollen Bread

This German Christmas bread, filled with dried fruits and marzipan, is shaped to resemble baby Jesus wrapped in a blanket, adding a sweet touch of symbolism.

20. Pomegranates for Decoration

In South Africa, where Christmas falls in the summer, pomegranates are used to decorate Christmas meals. Bright red pomegranate seeds add a splash of festive color to dishes.

21. Ghost Story Feasts in Victorian England

In Victorian England, it was a tradition to tell ghost stories during Christmas feasts. Imagine having roast duck while hearing a spooky tale—definitely an unusual pairing!

22. Fruitcake That Lasts Forever

Traditional fruitcakes, if stored properly, can last for years without going bad! It's even joked about as the Christmas gift that keeps on giving, whether you want it to or not.

23. Eggnog

Eggnog started in medieval England as a warm, spiced milk drink called "posset"—it was the go-to drink for fancy celebrations. When eggnog made its way to America, it became a popular holiday treat, especially with a dash of rum for adults!

24. Eggnog for the president

George Washington even had his own recipe for eggnog, which included brandy, whiskey, and rum—talk about festive!

25. The lucky mince pie

In England, it's said that eating a mince pie each day of the 12 Days of Christmas brings good luck for the year—better get munching!

26. Illegal pie

Mince pies were once banned by Oliver Cromwell in the 17th century because they were considered too indulgent—glad that didn't last!

27. Christmas Pudding: A Steamed Delight

Coins or charms are often hidden in the pudding, and finding one in your slice means you'll have good fortune.

28. Giant Stollen

Stollen is a traditional German Christmas bread filled with dried fruits, nuts, and marzipan, and dusted with powdered sugar. The city of Dresden holds an annual Stollen Festival, where they bake a giant stollen that weighs over 4,000 pounds!

29. Panettone: Italy's Tall Treat

Panettone is a sweet Italian bread that's tall and fluffy, filled with raisins and candied fruit. It originated in Milan, and it's said that a young baker invented it to impress his love— it's a romantic Christmas story!

30. Longest Christmas Stollen Ever

The longest Christmas stollen ever baked measured an incredible 236 feet long! It was made by Lidl in the Netherlands at Haarlem Railway Station on December 10, 2010. The stollen took 2.5 hours to prepare and another 2.5 hours to bake—all as one gigantic piece!

31. Christmas in the Sun: Australia

In Australia, Christmas falls in the middle of summer, so many families celebrate with a barbecue or a beach picnic. The traditional meal features seafood like prawns and lobster, along with cold salads to stay cool.

32. Feast of the Seven Fishes in Italy

On Christmas Eve, Italian families celebrate with the Feast of the Seven Fishes—a delicious meal featuring multiple seafood dishes that's a highlight of the holiday celebration.

33. Iceland's Traditional Christmas Meal

In Iceland, the traditional Christmas meal often includes smoked lamb, potatoes, and a special bread called "laufabrauð," which is thin and intricately patterned.

34. Noche Buena Feast

On Christmas Eve, known as "Noche Buena," families gather for a festive feast featuring dishes like lechon (roast pig), ham, and sweet rice cakes.

35. Fried Chicken Christmas in Japan

Christmas isn't a traditional holiday in Japan, but thanks to a clever marketing campaign in the 1970s, eating fried chicken has become a popular Christmas tradition. Many families order their KFC Christmas meal weeks in advance!

36. Christmas Pudding Started as a Soup

Back in the 1300s, Christmas pudding wasn't

the rich, fruity dessert we know today—it was actually called 'frumenty' and looked like a soup! Made from beef, mutton, fruit, wine, and spices, it was eaten before Christmas so people wouldn't be too full for the big feast on Christmas Day.

37. A Pig's Head for Christmas Dinner

Before turkey became the star of the Christmas feast, it was traditional to serve a pig's head with mustard as the main dish. Turkey didn't make an appearance on the Christmas menu until King Henry VIII popularized it in the 1500s. Imagine seeing a pig's head as your festive centerpiece!

38. Kūčios: A Lithuanian Feast

In Lithuania, Christmas Eve is celebrated with a traditional feast called Kūčios, featuring twelve dishes that symbolize the twelve apostles. These dishes are all meat-free, often including herring, beet soup, and special grain dishes.

39. Norwegian Rice Porridge

In Norway, a popular Christmas dish is "risgrøt" or rice porridge, served with sugar, cinnamon, and butter. A single almond is hidden in the porridge, and whoever finds it is said to have good luck for the upcoming year.

40. Portuguese Bolo Rei

In Portugal, people enjoy "Bolo Rei" or King's Cake during the Christmas season. This colorful cake is filled with dried fruits and nuts, and traditionally, a small charm and a fava bean are hidden inside. Whoever finds the charm gets good luck, but finding the bean means you have to buy next year's cake!

Chapter 4

STRANGE CHRISTMAS AROUND THE WORLD

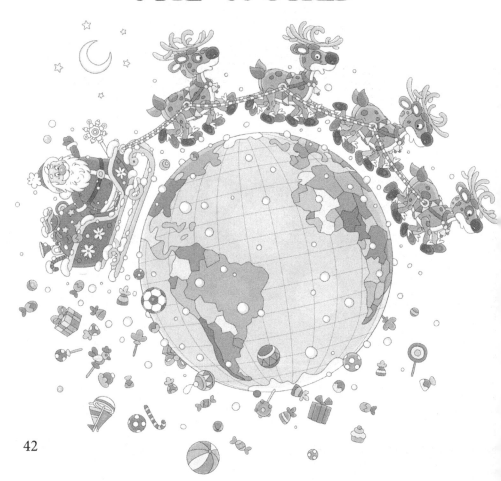

1. The World's Longest Christmas List

The world's longest Christmas wish list was over 13,000 feet long—it took over an hour just to unroll!

2. Scandinavian Gift Goat

In Scandinavia, people once believed that a goat brought presents on Christmas Day instead of Santa Claus.

3. World's Largest Elf Gathering

A total of 1,762 participants set the record for the largest gathering of people dressed as Christmas elves—holiday spirit at its finest!

4. Snowman Festival in Japan

In Sapporo, Japan, people build over 10,000 snowmen each year as part of an ice festival—a true snowman wonderland!

5. Snow Angels World Record

In 2007, a group of 8,962 people simultaneously made snow angels in North Dakota, USA—what a sight!

6. Christmas Underwater

Did you know that in the Maldives, some people celebrate Christmas underwater? Resorts there offer scuba diving experiences where guests can decorate submerged Christmas trees and even exchange gifts while surrounded by colorful fish—talk about a unique holiday celebration!

7. Christmas Markets on Boats

In Thailand, they celebrate Christmas with unique "floating markets." Vendors decorate their boats with Christmas lights and sell festive treats while gliding along the river, creating a magical atmosphere where you can shop for gifts right on the water!

8. Nutcracker Museum

A nutcracker museum in Kansas has more than 6,000 nutcrackers—plenty of festive soldiers for the holiday season.

9. Donald Duck Christmas Tradition in Sweden

In Sweden, it's a Christmas Eve tradition to watch a particular Donald Duck cartoon called "Donald Duck and His Friends Wish You a Merry Christmas". This tradition started in the 1960s, and every year, families gather around the TV at 3 PM to watch it—it's one of the most beloved parts of their holiday celebration.

10. Christmas Once Banned in Scotland

Christmas was banned in Scotland for nearly 400 years! In the 16th century, John Knox, a Scottish religious reformer, banned Christmas celebrations because he believed only holidays explicitly mentioned in the Bible should be observed—and Christmas wasn't one of them. Christmas only became an official public holiday in Scotland in 1958. Before that, people mostly celebrated Hogmanay on New Year's Eve.

11. Iceland's Christmas Book Flood

In Iceland, Christmas Eve is known for a special tradition called "Jólabókaflóð," or the Christmas Book Flood. On this night, people exchange books and spend the rest of the evening cozied up with hot cocoa and a good read. It's a holiday that's all about stories and quality time!

12. The Longest Christmas in the World

Christmas celebrations in the Philippines are among the longest in the world, starting in September and stretching all the way to January. Filipinos get into the festive spirit for nearly a third of the year, with decorations, songs, and celebrations lasting for months.

13. Hide the Pickle Tradition in America

In America, many families play the "hide the pickle" game. A glass pickle ornament is hidden somewhere on the Christmas tree, and whoever finds it first on Christmas Day gets an extra present. Although the origins are unclear—some say it started in Germany, but there's no proof—it's a quirky tradition that adds a bit of fun competition to the holiday.

14. Christmas Eve Celebrations in Peru

In Peru, Christmas Day is celebrated on Christmas Eve, known as "La Noche Buena" or "The Good Night." After attending church, families enjoy a big festive feast, open presents, and stay up until midnight to celebrate together. It's a night filled with joy and togetherness.

15. The Nativity Scene in Italy

In Italy, the nativity scene, or "presepe," is a popular Christmas decoration. Many families create their own elaborate versions, often including detailed figurines, lights, and miniature settings. It's a tradition that brings the story of Christmas to life in Italian homes.

16. Nikolaustag in Germany

In Germany, St. Nicholas visits children on December 6th, a day known as "Nikolaustag." Children leave their shoes out the night before, and in the morning, they find them filled with small gifts, candies, and treats left by St. Nicholas. It's an early start to the Christmas festivities that kids look forward to every year!

17. Christmas Illuminations in Japan

In Japan, instead of focusing on Santa Claus, many people celebrate the Christmas season with breathtaking light displays called "illuminations." These dazzling displays fill the winter nights with festive colors, turning cities into beautiful wonderlands.

18. Las Posadas in Mexico

In Mexico, Christmas celebrations begin on December 16th with "Las Posadas." This tradition reenacts Mary and Joseph's search for shelter. For nine nights, people go door-to-door in a procession, singing and asking for a place to stay, just like Mary and Joseph did.

19. Epiphany Gifts in Mexico

On January 6th, Mexican children receive gifts from the "Three Wise Men" in celebration of Epiphany. It's a tradition that marks the end of the holiday season and celebrates the visit of the Wise Men to baby Jesus.

20. The 13 Yule Lads of Iceland

In Iceland, children are visited by the 13 Yule Lads leading up to Christmas. Each Yule Lad has a mischievous personality, like Spoon-Licker or Door-Slammer, and they leave small gifts in children's shoes. It's a quirky and fun tradition that makes the countdown to Christmas full of surprises!

21. Christmas Sunshine in Australia

In Australia, Christmas happens in the middle of summer, which means plenty of sunshine instead of snow! Santa Claus is often seen in shorts, and he might even surf the waves—Christmas Down Under is all about celebrating in the summer heat!

22. St. Lucia's Day in Sweden

In Sweden, Christmas celebrations kick off on December 13th with St. Lucia's Day. On this day, girls dress in white robes and wear crowns of candles, leading processions that bring warmth and light to the dark winter days.

23. The Gävle Goat of Sweden

Every year in the Swedish town of Gävle, a giant straw goat, known as the Gävle Goat, is built as part of the Christmas celebrations. However, it's gained fame for another reason— pranksters often burn it down, turning the goat into a target for mischief!

24. The Giant Lantern Festival in the Philippines

The Philippines hosts the Giant Lantern Festival each year in the city of San Fernando, known as the "Christmas Capital of the Philippines." The festival features enormous lanterns made with thousands of lights, symbolizing hope and the festive spirit - it's truly a magical sight!

25. Santa's Official Hometown in Finland

In Finland, Santa Claus is said to live in Rovaniemi, located in the Arctic Circle. This magical place is even known as Santa's official hometown! Families can visit Santa's Village, meet Santa himself, and cross the Arctic Circle—it's like stepping right into Santa's winter wonderland!

26. Lighting Candles on Christmas Eve in Finland

In Finland, it's a heartfelt tradition to visit the graves of loved ones on Christmas Eve. Families light candles at the graves, creating a peaceful and beautiful glow that fills the cemeteries, making it a truly touching part of the holiday season.

27. The Mischievous Nisse in Norway

In Norway, there's a fun Christmas tradition involving "Nisse," the Christmas gnome. Families leave out a bowl of porridge for the Nisse, and if they forget, the little gnome might get naughty and play tricks on them! It's a way of keeping the Nisse happy and avoiding any holiday mischief.

28. "Strong Water" Tradition in Serbia

In Serbia, there's a special "strong water" tradition on Christmas morning. Girls and women collect water from a well, spring, or stream, believing that this water holds special powers. Drinking it is said to make them stronger and healthier for the coming year. It's a unique way of starting Christmas Day full of strength and positivity!

29. Recycled Bottle Light Show in Ohio

A family in Ohio designed a holiday light show using thousands of recycled plastic bottles, turning waste into stunning illuminated sculptures. The funds raised supported clean water initiatives.

30. Knitted Christmas Village in England

Knitters in England created a delightful "Knitted Christmas Village" featuring yarn-made houses and characters. The display raised donations for a charity providing warm clothing for the homeless.

31. Reverse Advent Calendar in Canada

In Canada, a community built a "Reverse Advent Calendar," encouraging visitors to donate food or clothing items each day, supporting local shelters during the holidays.

32. Origami Light Display in Scotland

Artists in Scotland decorated an entire street with illuminated origami figures, creating an enchanting stroll for visitors. Donations supported an art therapy program for children.

33. Hot Air Balloon Advent Calendar in France

Volunteers in France made an advent calendar from 24 illuminated miniature hot air balloons, each themed to a different country, celebrating cultures from around the world.

34. Florida's 70,000-Light Advent

A man in Florida decorated his house with 70,000 lights, creating a new Christmas scene every day during advent, delighting the local community.

35. The Pooping Figurine in Catalonia, Spain

In Catalonia, Spain, nativity scenes include a "Caganer," a figurine of a man pooping, hidden away in the back of the scene. It's a 200-year-old tradition loved by children.

36. Mashed Potato Christmas Trees in Japan

In Japan, some people make mashed potato Christmas trees, coloring them green and decorating with broccoli, carrots, and cheese stars—turning potatoes into festive fun.

37. Belgium's Record Carol Singers

In 2011, 15,000 people in Belgium sang Christmas carols together, setting the record for the largest group of carol singers.

38. The Battle of the Oranges in Sicily

In Palermo, Sicily, Christmas celebrations include "The Battle of the Oranges," a massive orange-throwing event like a snowball fight but with fruit.

39. Snowman Burning Day in America

March 20 is "Snowman Burning Day" in America, marking the end of winter and the beginning of spring by burning a snowman figure.

40. Christmas Stars in India

In India, people hang star-shaped lanterns for Christmas to bring good luck. Churches are adorned with poinsettias and candles for Midnight Mass.

Chapter 5

REINDEER AND WINTER ANIMALS

1. Reindeer Migration

Reindeer migrate more than 600 miles every year—that's about the distance from Paris, France, to Berlin, Germany!

2. Christmas Tree Worms

Christmas tree worms can live for more than 40 years and are named for their tree-like shape. They bring a little underwater Christmas spirit to the ocean!

3. Male Snowy Owls

Male snowy owls get whiter as they age, which helps them blend in with the snowy landscape.

4. Wood Frogs' Winter Trick

When wood frogs hibernate, about two-thirds of their body water turns to ice—they become little froggy ice cubes!

5. Reindeer Strength

Reindeer, famed for their association with pulling Santa's sleigh, are powerful animals that can pull a load of up to 300 pounds at an average of eight miles per hour.

6. Reindeer and Caribou

Reindeer are called "caribou" in North America, but they're the same species—just with different names depending on where they live.

7. Santa's Reindeer Are Female

Santa's reindeer must be female because male reindeer shed their antlers in winter, while females keep theirs. So, those antlered sleigh-pullers are all ladies!

8. Reindeer Snowshoe Hooves

Reindeer have special hooves that work like snowshoes, making it easier for them to walk on snow and ice.

9. Double Fur for Warmth

Reindeer have a second layer of fur to stay warm in freezing temperatures—keeping them cozy in the cold.

10. Swimming Reindeer

Reindeer are excellent swimmers and often cross rivers and lakes during their migrations.

11. Rudolph's Red Nose

Rudolph's nose might be magic, but real reindeer noses turn reddish in winter to help regulate their temperature in the cold.

12. Seasonal Eye Color

Reindeer eyes change color with the seasons—from gold in summer to blue in winter—helping them see better in different light conditions.

13. Reindeer Names

The names of Santa's reindeer come from the poem "The Night Before Christmas," but originally, "Donner" and "Blitzen" were called "Dunder" and "Blixem," meaning thunder and lightning in Dutch.

14. UV Vision Superpower

Reindeer are one of the few mammals that can see ultraviolet light. This unique ability helps them spot predators and food against the bright, reflective snow and ice, making them perfectly adapted to their Arctic environment.

15. Reindeer Love Mushrooms

Reindeer are known to eat Amanita muscaria, a red-and-white mushroom that's actually toxic to many animals. The mushroom causes them to become slightly "high," which some researchers think may help reindeer tolerate the cold better or ward off parasites.

16. Largest Land Carnivores

Polar bears are the largest land carnivores, weighing up to 1,500 pounds—heavier than a grand piano! Their thick fat and dense fur help keep them warm in the icy Arctic.

17. Black Skin and Transparent Fur

Polar bears have black skin under their fur to absorb heat, and their fur is actually transparent, reflecting light to make them look white.

18. Incredible Swimmers

Polar bears are great swimmers and can swim for days in search of food. They mainly eat seals, hunting them near ice holes where seals come up for air.

19. Superb Sense of Smell

Polar bears have an excellent sense of smell and can detect a seal from miles away.

20. Cubs Stay Close

Polar bear cubs stay with their mothers for about two years before venturing out on their own.

21. A Celebration of Bears

A group of polar bears is called a "celebration"—a fittingly festive term for these majestic animals.

22. Marine Mammals

Polar bears are considered marine mammals because they spend much of their lives on sea ice and swimming in the ocean.

23. Large White Owls

Snowy owls are one of the largest owl species, known for their bright white feathers. Unlike most owls, they're active during the day, especially during the Arctic's 24-hour summer daylight.

24. Lemming Lovers

Snowy owls mainly eat small mammals like lemmings, and one owl can eat over 1,600 lemmings in a year!

25. Male vs. Female Feathers

Male snowy owls are whiter than females, while females have more dark spots to blend in while nesting.

26. Migrating South

Snowy owls migrate south for winter, sometimes reaching the northern United States. A group of snowy owls is called a "parliament"—just like a gathering of wise leaders!

27. Seasonal Fur Changes

Arctic foxes have thick fur that changes with the seasons—white in winter to blend with the snow and brown in summer to match the tundra.

28. Fluffy Tail Blanket

Their fluffy tails act like a blanket, keeping them warm while they sleep.

29. Small Ears for the Cold

Arctic foxes have small ears to reduce heat loss, helping them survive extremely cold temperatures as low as -50°F.

30. Scavenger Lifestyle

Arctic foxes are scavengers and often follow polar bears to eat leftover scraps.

31. Generational Dens

They build dens in the ground and may use the same den for generations.

32. Large Litters

Arctic foxes have litters of up to 14 pups, making them one of the most prolific mammals in the Arctic.

33. Penguins of the Southern Hemisphere

Penguins live in the Southern Hemisphere, with emperor penguins famously residing in Antarctica. Though they can't fly, penguins are expert swimmers, using their flippers to "fly" underwater.

34. Tallest Penguins

Emperor penguins are the tallest penguin species, reaching up to 4 feet. To stay warm, they huddle in large groups, taking turns being on the outside of the huddle.

35. Egg-Balancing Dads

Male emperor penguins keep the egg warm by balancing it on their feet, while the female goes hunting. They keep it off the ice to ensure it stays cozy.

36. Blubber Layer

Penguins have a layer of fat called "blubber" that keeps them warm in the icy waters.

37. Underwater Hunters

Penguins can stay underwater for up to 20 minutes while hunting for fish.

38. Fluffy Chicks

Baby penguins, called chicks, are covered in soft down feathers until they grow their waterproof adult feathers.

39. Tobogganing on Ice

Penguins slide on their bellies across the ice—a movement called "tobogganing"—to move quickly and save energy.

40. Tuxedo Camouflage

Penguins' black and white "tuxedo" coloring is called counter-shading, which helps them camouflage from predators while swimming.

Chapter 6

SNOWY ADVENTURES AND WINTER MYTHS

1. Blue Snowflakes

Snow sometimes appears blue, especially in deep drifts where light is filtered—turning winter into a magical blue landscape.

2. Every Snowflake Is Unique

No two snowflakes are exactly alike. Each snowflake has a unique structure due to the way water molecules arrange themselves as they freeze—making each one a tiny, intricate work of art!

3. Snow Can Be Different Colors

Though we usually think of snow as white, it can also appear in colors like pink, blue, or even green. This is often due to algae or impurities in the snow, like "watermelon snow," which turns pink due to algae containing a red pigment.

4. Snow Isn't Actually White

Snow appears white, but it's actually made up of clear ice crystals. The white appearance comes from how the light is scattered by the many surfaces of the ice crystals, reflecting all colors and making it look white.

5. Snowflakes Have Six Sides

Snowflakes almost always have six sides or branches, thanks to the way water molecules form hexagonal patterns when they freeze. It's why snowflakes are famous for their beautiful, six-pointed symmetry.

6. It Can Be Too Cold to Snow

Snow forms when moisture in the air freezes, but when temperatures drop too low, there's often not enough moisture for snow to form. So, in extremely cold places, it might actually be too cold to snow!

7. The Largest Snowflake Ever Recorded

According to reports, the largest snowflake ever observed measured 15 inches wide and 8 inches thick. This gigantic flake was spotted in Montana in 1887, though it's hard to verify due to the long time ago!

8. Snow Insulates Against Cold

Snow is actually a great insulator. Igloos, made from compacted snow, can stay quite warm inside due to the trapped air between the snow crystals, which helps keep heat in and the cold out.

9. Snow's Weight Can Be Surprising

A cubic foot of fresh snow can weigh as little as 3 pounds, but if compacted or wet, that same cubic foot can weigh as much as 20 pounds. This explains why shoveling heavy, wet snow can be such a workout!

10. The Sound of Silence

Fresh snow absorbs sound, which is why everything feels quieter after a snowfall. The air pockets between the snowflakes trap sound waves, creating that peaceful, muffled effect.

11. Snowball Fight Record

Around 8,200 people participated in a massive snowball fight in Saskatchewan, Canada—a true winter wonderland battle!

12. World's Biggest Snowstorm

A single snowstorm can drop 40 million tons of snow, transforming the landscape into a winter wonderland overnight.

13. Longest Ice-Skating Trail

The longest ice-skating trail on Earth stretches 18 miles in British Columbia, Canada—perfect for a day of skating!

14. Thunder Snow

During some intense snowstorms, lightning and thunder can occur—a phenomenon known as "thundersnow." It's similar to a regular thunderstorm but happens in a winter setting. Thundersnow is rare and fascinating, with thunder muffled by the blanket of snow.

15. Snowstorms vs. Blizzards

Not all snowstorms are blizzards. For a snowstorm to be classified as a blizzard, it must have winds of at least 35 mph, visibility reduced to less than a quarter of a mile, and these conditions must last for at least three hours.

16. Snowfall Speed

Snowflakes generally fall at a speed of 1 to 6 feet per second, which is relatively slow, giving them their signature graceful descent. The speed can be influenced by flake size, wind, and other weather conditions.

17. Snow Drifts Can Tower Over Homes

Wind during snowstorms can cause snow drifts that tower over houses. In extreme cases, drifts can reach heights of over 20 feet, completely burying homes and buildings.

18. Snowstorms Can Cover Entire Countries

The Great Blizzard of 1888 in the United States was one of the largest snowstorms ever, affecting the entire East Coast. It dropped up to 50 inches of snow in some areas and even caused snowdrifts as high as 50 feet, impacting everything from transportation to basic services.

19. Snowstorms Can Happen Without Freezing Temperatures

Believe it or not, snow can still fall when temperatures are above freezing. If the air is just slightly above 32°F (0°C), snow can still reach the ground, especially if the air higher up in the atmosphere is cold enough.

20. Whiteout Conditions

Snowstorms can create "whiteout" conditions, where blowing snow drastically reduces visibility. In severe cases, it can become impossible to see anything beyond a few feet, making travel extremely dangerous.

21. Snowstorms in Deserts

It's rare, but snowstorms can happen in desert areas. The Sahara Desert, for instance, experienced snow in 2018. While the snow didn't last long, it was an amazing sight to see sand dunes dusted in white!

22. Lake-Effect Snowstorms

Lake-effect snowstorms occur when cold air moves over warmer lake waters, picking up moisture and dropping it as heavy snow downwind of the lake. This phenomenon is common around the Great Lakes in North America and can create astonishing amounts of snow in localized areas.

23. Snowstorms Can Cause Avalanches

Heavy snowstorms can lead to avalanches in mountainous areas. When large amounts of snow accumulate on unstable slopes, it can lead to sudden snow slides that cascade down the mountain, causing significant destruction.

24. Oldest Winter Sport

Skiing is one of the oldest winter sports, with evidence of people skiing as far back as 6,000 years ago in what is now China and Scandinavia. Skis were originally used as a practical way to travel across snowy landscapes.

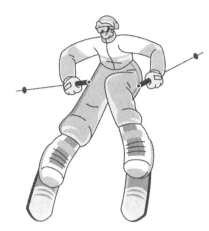

25. Snowboarding Was Inspired by Surfing

Snowboarding was created in the 1960s by combining elements of surfing, skateboarding, and skiing. Early snowboards were called "snurfers" (snow-surfers) and were made from a single plank without bindings.

26. Olympic Ski Jumping Distance

Ski jumpers at the Olympics can fly over 800 feet, the length of more than two football fields! The world record for the longest ski jump is over 830 feet (253.5 meters) - an incredible distance to glide through the air.

27. Speed Skating Thrills

Speed skating is all about racing across the ice as fast as possible - skaters can reach speeds of up to 35 miles per hour!

28. Skeleton: The Face-First Sledding Sport

Skeleton is an intense winter sport where athletes ride a small sled headfirst down an icy track at speeds of up to 80 mph (130 km/h). It gets its name from the skeletal-like appearance of the early sleds.

29. Heli-Skiing for Ultimate Adventure

Heli-skiing involves being flown by helicopter to remote mountain peaks to ski down untouched powder. It's one of the most extreme forms of skiing, offering adventurers the chance to ski where no lift can take them.

30. Norway's Young Skiers

In Norway, skiing is such an important part of the culture that children often learn to ski as soon as they can walk. It's not uncommon to see tiny skiers hitting the slopes—talk about starting young!

31. Ski Goggles for Sun Protection

Skiers wear special goggles to protect their eyes from the bright glare caused by sunlight reflecting off the snow. The intense light can be harsh, and the goggles help keep their vision clear and safe.

32. Ice Skating's Finnish Origins

Ice skating started in Finland over 4,000 years ago! Early skates were made from animal bones tied to the feet. Today, ice skaters use sharp metal blades to glide and make precise carving movements to change direction on the ice.

33. Ice Skating's Dutch Beginnings

The Dutch are credited with making ice skating a popular pastime in the 13th century. They used frozen canals to skate for fun and as a way to get around during winter.

34. Speed Skiing Is Super Fast

Speed skiing is the fastest non-motorized sport on Earth, with skiers reaching speeds of over 150 mph (240 km/h). These athletes wear aerodynamic helmets and suits to minimize air resistance as they fly downhill.

35. World's Largest Ice Rink

The largest ice rink in the world is located in Ottawa, Canada, stretching nearly five miles along the Rideau Canal. It's a favorite spot for skaters during the winter.

36. Wild Skating Adventures

Skating on natural ice is called "wild skating." It's popular in places like Sweden and the Netherlands, where lakes freeze over in winter, offering perfect conditions for skating in nature.

37. Yukigassen: Japan's Snowball Fight Tournament

In Japan, there's an annual snowball fight tournament called "Yukigassen," where teams compete to become the ultimate snowball champions.

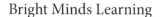

38. Record Snowball Fight in Seattle

The biggest snowball fight on record took place in Seattle, Washington, with over 5,800 participants. That's a lot of snowballs flying through the air!

Imagine This!

Picture a snowball fight with hundreds of kids from around the world. What would your strategy be to win? Would you build a super tall snow fort or make snowballs as fast as possible?

39. World's Tallest Snowwoman

The largest snowman ever built was actually a snowwoman named Olympia, standing 122 feet tall in Maine, USA—about as tall as a 10-story building!

40. Snow Lanterns to Light the Night

In some places, people make "snow lanterns" by packing snow into shapes and placing candles inside. It's a beautiful way to light up a winter night.

41. Quebec Winter Carnival

In Canada, the Quebec Winter Carnival is a massive celebration featuring parades, ice canoe races, and a giant ice palace—it's all about having fun in the cold!

42. Reindeer Racing in Norway

Norway hosts a reindeer racing festival where participants race through the snow pulled by reindeer—a unique and thrilling way to enjoy winter!

43. Midsummer Christmas in Sweden

In Sweden, people celebrate "Midsummer Christmas" in July, enjoying a second Christmas under the warm summer sun.

44. World Ice Art Championships in Alaska

The World Ice Art Championships are held in Alaska, where artists carve amazing sculptures from giant blocks of ice—an impressive winter showcase!

45. Elfstedentocht Ice Skating Race

The Netherlands has "Elfstedentocht," an ice skating race across 11 cities that only happens when the canals freeze—a rare and exciting event!

46. Finland's Snow Castle

In Finland, a snow castle is built every year, complete with ice furniture and even an ice hotel for adventurous guests who want to spend the night in this frosty wonderland.

47. Snow Roller Phenomenon

Snow rollers are a rare natural phenomenon where the wind pushes chunks of snow, causing them to roll across the ground and form cylinder-like shapes —like nature's version of snowballs, but much larger!

48. Ski Resorts in the Desert

The Mall of the Emirates in Dubai has an indoor ski resort called "Ski Dubai," complete with real snow, a ski slope, and even penguins. It's one of the few places in the world where you can experience snow sports in the middle of the desert.

49. Ski Ballet: The Forgotten Sport

In the 1980s and 1990s, ski ballet was a competitive winter sport that combined skiing with dance moves, flips, and spins. It was once part of the freestyle skiing competitions, but the unique mix of skiing and choreography never gained enough popularity to remain mainstream.

50. Ice Marathons

In Antarctica, there's an annual "Ice Marathon" where participants run 26.2 miles in freezing temperatures across snow and ice. It's one of the world's most challenging marathons, testing the endurance of even the most experienced runners.

Chapter 7

ANTARCTICA AND THE WONDERS OF THE WINTER WORLD

1. Scientists on Floating Ice

Scientists at the North Pole work on floating research stations—it's a chilly but fascinating place to study the world!

2. Permanent Ice and Snow

About 12% of the Earth is covered in permanent ice and snow, mostly found in Antarctica and the Arctic.

3. Four North Poles

Did you know there are actually four North Poles? There's the geographic North Pole, the magnetic North Pole, the geomagnetic North Pole, and the pole of inaccessibility.

4. Snow Globe Invention

The snow globe was actually invented by accident when an inventor was trying to make a brighter light bulb. Now, it's a beloved holiday decoration!

5. Constant Daylight and Darkness at the North Pole

The North Pole experiences six months of constant daylight and six months of constant darkness due to its proximity to the Earth's axis and the planet's tilt.

6. A Floating Ice Cap

The North Pole is a floating ice cap that moves around, shifting about 4 inches per year. There's no land there, with the nearest land over 400 miles away.

7. Every Direction is South

At the magnetic North Pole, every direction points south. The magnetic North Pole is slightly different from the true North Pole, and it moves over time.

8. Lomonosov Ridge

The North Pole is home to an underwater mountain range called the Lomonosov Ridge, adding some mystery beneath the Arctic ice.

9. Astronaut Training at the North Pole

The North Pole is considered an extreme environment, making it a testing ground for astronauts preparing for space missions.

10. No Time Zone

There's no official time zone at the North Pole—it's either all hours or no hours, depending on the season.

11. North Pole Marathon

The North Pole Marathon costs $15,500 to compete, including flights to the icy region. Participants run in some of the most extreme conditions on Earth.

12. Antarctica: The Icy Desert

Despite being covered in ice, Antarctica is technically a desert because of its lack of precipitation, making it the world's largest ice desert.

13. Fresh Water Reserve

Antarctica's ice holds about 70% of the world's fresh water, making it a massive frozen reservoir.

14. Walk Around the World

At the South Pole in Antarctica, you can walk around the entire world by just taking a few steps, as all lines of longitude converge there.

15. No Permanent Residents

Antarctica has no native human population—only researchers and scientists live there temporarily.

16. All Day or All Night

In Antarctica, the winter brings six months of darkness, while the summer has six months of continuous daylight—either all day or all night!

17. Coldest Temperature on Earth

The coldest temperature ever recorded on Earth was in Antarctica at -144°F, which is even colder than the surface of Mars!

18. Antarctica's Fierce Winds

Winds in Antarctica can reach over 200 mph, creating blizzards that last for days and making it one of the windiest places on Earth.

19. Antarctic Ice History

The Antarctic ice sheet is millions of years old, and scientists study it to learn about Earth's climate history and past environmental changes.

20. Emperor Penguins: Antarctica's Winter Residents

Emperor penguins, standing about 4 feet tall, are the largest penguin species and the most famous residents of Antarctica. They are the only animals that stay through Antarctica's harsh winter, huddling together to keep warm.

21. Playful Adelie Penguins

Adelie penguins are also found in Antarctica and are known for their playful, curious nature, adding a bit of charm to the icy continent.

22. Seals of Antarctica

Several species of seals call Antarctica home, including the Weddell seal and the fierce leopard seal. Leopard seals are predators with powerful jaws and spotted coats, making them formidable hunters in the Antarctic waters.

23. Krill: The Foundation of the Antarctic Food Chain

Antarctic krill, tiny shrimp-like creatures, play a crucial role in the ecosystem. They are the primary food source for many Antarctic animals, including seals and blue whales—the largest animals on Earth—that visit Antarctica to feast on the abundance of krill.

24. Wandering Albatross: Masters of the Antarctic Skies

The wandering albatross, with an impressive wingspan of up to 11 feet, is one of the majestic birds that soar over Antarctica's icy waters, gliding effortlessly for long distances.

25. Orcas in Antarctic Waters

Orcas, also known as killer whales, are often spotted in the waters around Antarctica. They are skilled hunters, preying on seals and fish, and are a powerful presence in the icy seas.

26. Antarctic Silverfish: Survivors of the Cold

Antarctic silverfish are one of the few fish species that live in these frigid waters. They have special proteins in their blood that prevent them from freezing, allowing them to thrive in extreme conditions.

27. Discovery of Antarctica

Antarctica was the last continent to be discovered, with the first confirmed sighting made in 1820 by a Russian expedition.

28. Ernest Shackleton's Survival Story

One of the most famous Antarctic explorers was Ernest Shackleton, who led a daring expedition in 1914. His ship, the Endurance, became trapped in the ice, but Shackleton and his crew managed to survive against all odds—one of the greatest survival stories of all time.

29. Race to the South Pole

Norwegian explorer Roald Amundsen was the first person to reach the South Pole in 1911, beating British explorer Robert

Falcon Scott by just a few weeks. Amundsen used sled dogs for the journey, while Scott's team used ponies, which struggled in the harsh conditions.

30. The Antarctic Treaty

The Antarctic Treaty, signed in 1959, ensures that Antarctica is used only for peaceful purposes and scientific research, preserving it as a place for discovery rather than conflict.

31. First Woman in Antarctica

Caroline Mikkelsen, a Norwegian explorer, became the first woman to set foot on Antarctica in 1935, paving the way for future female explorers.

32. World's Southernmost Post Office

Antarctica is home to the world's southernmost post office, where tourists can send postcards from the bottom of the world— making for a unique memento!

33. Shifting South Pole Marker

The geographic South Pole is marked by a small sign and a striped pole, but it shifts about 30 feet each year due to the movement of the thick ice beneath it.

34. Ceremonial South Pole

There's also a ceremonial South Pole, surrounded by flags of the Antarctic Treaty nations. This is the iconic spot where most visitors take their photos.

35. Amundsen-Scott South Pole Station

The Amundsen-Scott South Pole Station is a research facility located at the South Pole, operating year-round despite the extreme cold and isolation.

36. Extreme Cold

During winter, temperatures at the South Pole can drop below -100°F, making it one of the harshest and most inhospitable places on Earth.

37. High-Altitude Adventure

The South Pole sits atop a plateau of ice about 9,000 feet above sea level, making it a high-altitude adventure for those who visit.

38. Ice Thickness and Movement

The ice at the South Pole is more than 9,000 feet thick and slowly moves, carrying the physical South Pole marker along with it year after year.

39. South Pole Telescope

The South Pole Telescope is used to study cosmic microwave background radiation, which helps scientists learn more about the early universe and the origins of cosmic structures.

40. Ozone Hole Discovery

In the 1970s, scientists discovered a hole in the ozone layer above Antarctica, leading to international agreements and efforts to protect the ozone layer.

41. Mount Erebus: The Southernmost Active Volcano

Antarctica has active volcanoes, including Mount Erebus, the southernmost active volcano in the world, constantly reminding us that even the coldest place on Earth has fiery activity beneath the surface.

42. Blood Falls: Antarctica's Bleeding Glacier

Blood Falls is a strange natural phenomenon where red-colored water flows out of a glacier, making it look like the ice is bleeding—caused by iron-rich water oxidizing when it hits the air.

43. McMurdo Dry Valleys: Polar Desert

The McMurdo Dry Valleys are some of the driest places on Earth, with almost no snow or ice, resembling a polar desert in the middle of Antarctica.

44. Newest Named Ocean

The Southern Ocean, which surrounds Antarctica, was officially recognized in 2000, making it the newest named ocean on Earth.

45. Massive Antarctic Icebergs

Icebergs breaking off from Antarctica can be enormous— one, named B-15, was larger than the entire island of Jamaica, a true giant floating on the ocean.

46. Heavy Ice Pushes Down the Land

The ice in Antarctica is so heavy that it actually compresses the land beneath it, pushing it down by several hundred feet due to its immense weight.

47. Hidden Ice Caves

Antarctica is home to ice caves that form when warm air from volcanic activity melts the ice from below, creating intricate and hidden tunnels beneath the surface.

48. Antarctic Algae Blooms

During the summer, parts of Antarctica are covered in bright green and orange algae, adding unexpected splashes of color to the stark, icy landscape.

49. Antarctica's Waterfall Under the Ice

Antarctica has a subglacial lake called Lake Vostok buried beneath over two miles of ice. It remains liquid due to geothermal heat and has been isolated from the rest of the world for millions of years, making it a unique ecosystem that could harbor unknown forms of life.

50. Antarctica's Singing Ice

Antarctica's ice can actually "sing"! The winds blowing over the ice sheets create vibrations that produce eerie, low-frequency sounds, almost like the ice is humming. This natural music gives scientists clues about the condition of the ice and changes in the environment.

Hi there, Amazing Reader!

Thank you for joining us in exploring so many amazing facts and trivia for this Christmas!

If you had as much fun reading as we did creating it, we'd love to hear your thoughts.

Reviews help other readers discover the book and let us know what you enjoyed the most. Whether it's a favorite pun, a corny joke or just the overall experience, your feedback means the world to us.

So, if you have a moment, please leave a review and share the Christmas fun with others!

Scan this QR Code to leave a review!

To thank you, there are some bonuses waiting for you.

Simply scan this QR Code to unlock them!

CONCLUSION

As you turn the last page of this book, don't let the curiosity end here! There's a whole world of incredible facts and fun waiting for you.

If you enjoyed this journey, why not keep the fun going?

Discover more awesome books from Bright Minds Learning that will spark your imagination and keep the fun going.

Scan the QR code below or search Bright Minds Learning on Amazon to explore our full collection and find your next adventure!

Made in United States
Orlando, FL
10 December 2024

55343423R00055